# CONFABULATIONS

*Poems*
*for*
*Malcolm Lowry*

*Sharon Thesen*

---

# CONFABULATIONS

---

*Poems
for
Malcolm Lowry*

*Oolichan Books*

Lantzville, British Columbia
1984

Among the sources are the *Selected Letters of Malcolm Lowry*, edited by
Harvey Breit and Margerie Bonner Lowry (J. P. Lippincott, 1965), *Under the
Volcano*, the stories in *Hear Us O Lord From Heaven Thy Dwelling Place*,
and Douglas Day's courageous biography entitled *Malcolm Lowry* (Oxford
University Press, 1973). Phrases taken directly from these sources are italicized,
except in poems where italics would have produced an undesired emphasis.
Images and situations, however, have been lifted, spliced, and grafted where
they were not just out-and-out invented. This, then, is not intended to be a
factual account of Malcolm Lowry's life.

Canadian Cataloguing in Publication Data

Thesen, Sharon, 1946-
Confabulations, poems for Malcolm Lowry

ISBN 0-88982-072-4

1. Lowry, Malcolm, 1909-1957, in fiction, drama,
poetry, etc.   I. Title.
PS8589.H47C6 1984        C811'.54        C84-091383-4
PR9199.3.T49C6 1984

Publication of this book has been financially assisted by the Canada Council
and by the Government of British Columbia through the British Columbia
Cultural Fund and the British Columbia Lottery Fund

Published by

OOLICHAN BOOKS
P.O. Box 10, Lantzville, B.C. VOR 2HO

Printed in Canada by

MORRISS PRINTING COMPANY LTD.
Victoria, British Columbia

*for Michael Ondaatje*

Clarence Malcolm Lowry is buried in the village of Ripe, in East Sussex, England, "just at the edge of the consecrated ground in the churchyard." He was 46 when he died. His body was found by his wife, Margerie, on the morning of June 27, 1957. Doctors and police meditated upon a broken gin bottle, a broken bottle of orange squash, and two empty bottles of sleeping pills, each having formerly contained approximately twenty-five three-grain sodium amytal tablets. Suicide was out of the question. A heart attack was considered likely, but the coroner, declaring it a "death by misadventure," testified at the inquest that Lowry's heart was perfectly sound, as were his liver and other organs.

I still believe that bad French wine was my nemesis. I began to improve slightly when I took to rum and gave up taking vitamins.

MALCOLM LOWRY, February 1949, Dollarton

When the fire devours itself, when the power turns against itself, it seems as if the whole being is made complete at the instant of its final ruin and the intensity of the destruction is the supreme proof, the clearest proof, of its existence.

GASTON BACHELARD, *The Psychoanalysis of Fire*

Malcolm Lowry
Late of the Bowery
His prose was flowery
And often glowery
He lived, nightly, and drank, daily,
And died playing the ukelele.

from *Selected Poems of Malcolm Lowry*

# CONFABULATIONS

*Poems
for
Malcolm Lowry*

A dove-grey morning
soon to turn blue
as lights go out
& silent movie begins
broken projector
flapping celluloid
mind's guts churning
sweating nervous erratic
guilt, it's okay
nothing wrong I could forget
it if I could remember it
legs & arms loosened out
mouth talking
fall back fast dissolve
a light snow falling in the room.

At the bottom of the garden
the hidden bottle. He makes
a rectitudinous beeline
for it, plain as day
his casualness an effort.
The heat spreading
everywhere, his mind
up to tricks his face
won't believe.
His stiff walk,
bones poisoned.
How he loves it all,
the amorous snake
in the amorous grass,
the disgusted neighbour
watering fruit trees
is his best friend.
The distant tequila the key
to the day, the beauty
of all things burning
through whitened glass,
his open heart
a surgical instrument.

Bacchus is not
the god in this case,
innocent & vulgar —
nor demon. Spirit
a magical language
binds community
sunders same.
Spirit resembling love
hence saboteur
of same. Sweet shortcut
to quote unquote hell
through a private
blinded paradise, *spiritus
contra spiritum.*

His ex-heart
speaking to the woman
they call the Blessed
Virgin is busy
making deals.
He's caught up in,
in love with
the exaltation
of the error
of his ways
outside the circle
outside the unmoved
& unmoving given.
He prays anyway
for love of life
at least, among
the flickering candles
beneath the serene
blue folds of her gown
his thick tongue
beating the words
behind his teeth:
*I have sunk low.*
*Let me sink lower still.*

White walls sweat flies
move fast as trains.

Gripping the counter's edge
to wait it out.

Watch the little maelstrom
in the draining sink,
the mindless unfaltering
laws-of-nature
vortex. *His steps
teetered to the left,
he could not make them
incline to the right.*

It was the dark.

The dark cantina
adjacent to the Bus Terminal
where lived
the widow Gregorio
and his debt
of five centavos.

Stooping over the half hidden
Tequila Anejo de Jalisco
& waving to the neighbour
he mentions the weather
& also
he's on the wagon.
The funeral wagon
I'd say, glares Mr. Quincey.
In any case
more sober when drunk
than sober.
There are three
standing on the balcony,
even the raggy sunflower
is erect & opprobrious.
He resents their
incessant nervous
watchfulness.
He's afraid
they think he's a liar.

The five attractive garter-snakes
assemble for the concert.
He's found their tastes
run to the gloomy.
His ukulele twanging out
hymn tunes
in diminished sevenths.
The pink grass swaying.
The clouds farting thunder.
The butterfly caught
in the jaws of the cat,
pulsing wings
frantic emerald curtains.

Should I say
Malcolm, your name
is the sound
of clam-tracks,
the knock of kelp
on rock? Or Clarence,
wooden matches hissing
at nightfall?

There you would be
sitting on the clam-hole beach
in the noonday sun
& two seconds later
your house is in flames.
Again. Manuscripts
& bottles of Bols gin
snatched from the hellfire
always at your heels
panting & fanged.

Correspondences
too creepy to ignore.
Or maybe just bad
ventilation, rotten
luck. You were right
about a lot of things —
*this world*
scissored your mind,
bone-dry shreds of ecstasy
& terror igniting
your fragile nests.

*Mea culpa.*
And the culprit
is my mother,
the nanny
who tried to smother me
one day on the cliff,
the Syphilis Museum
on Paradise Road,
my diseased eyes,
Bellevue where they put me,
my immense
imagination.
The only books in the house
*Inebriety* by Crabbe,
Conrad Aiken's *Blue Voyage*
(maybe two or three others.)
*Mea culpa.*
The doctor says
manic depressive, says
compulsive neurosis
the alcohol a mask.
Language the mask —
*pelado* — peeled —
now it takes me
up to a whole afternoon
to find the word
I need.

On the third boozeless day he rose,
virtue restored. Publishers
written to. A long, less
wibberley wobberley walk
along the beach rocks.
The delicate white haze
outside now, flattened zinc
coin of sea & sun a platinum
wavering disc.
Wharf creaking in the wake
of a tug, ferns
soaking up stones. The world
his oyster.
*"Welcome home," my wife
smiles, greeting me.
"Ah yes, my darling, it really is
home now. I love those curtains
you made."*

So why not a visit to our old friend
the bootlegger
on so fine an afternoon?

The dripping path grows
pitch black. Some dogs howl
at an absent moon, no drunk
tells time. A flashlight
beam from the dead
of night finds him sprawled
on the forest floor
gobbling ferns —

spitting spores
around the names
of constellations
crawling the sky.

He stands his back
to her, bare torso
outlined by sea & fir trees.
The callused tops of his hands
behind him kneading
& rubbing at the table top
he leans against,
3 packs a day voice
addressing the abyss
his wife writing it down.

The shakes so bad can't hold
a pen or pencil anymore
won't eat
needs help getting dressed

The writing body
flashing one-sided headache,
eczema on lower limbs,
heartbeat erratic,
weight loss,
blank dreams,
fatigue an invisible thief
peels away the days
at night alternating coma
& transmitter.

ferris wheel revolves
backward into black night
with Lowry the lone rider
vomiting mescal sideways
across the contrary circle
of fiesta-coloured lightbulbs

Where I am it is dark.

I fear the worst & alas my only friend
is the Virgin for those who have nobody with
& she is not much help.

I am being spied upon by 5 policemen
in black sunglasses. All day long
a vulture stares at me
from around the wash basin.
While I purify my sorrow.

Marquez shot to death
in a stupid drunken argument —
or no, They took Marquez
out of his house one afternoon
and shot him, saying *you no wrider*
*you an espider.*
At the time he was shaving
fresh from siesta his white shirt
on the back of a chair
rungs showing through like bones
& suddenly the dog barking —

They arrest me for drawing maps on the bar
with a finger dipped in tequila —
communist, agitator, spy — plus
no passport.

Ugly voices spatter the street
with vowels of *la mordida.*

In Mexican prisons the third degree
is castration. They tried that
one fine night, unsuccessfully
I regret to say.

Later we ended up in the *zocalo*
guards & all, roaring with mescal
& everyone with blue faces.

They are looking for me yet.
I practise knots
on the fringe of her yellow shawl
its softness on my legs
striped with bars of shuttered light.

That last night in the cantina
with Yvonne & Hugh, spectral chicken
on the day-of-the-dead menu
the glasses of mescal appear &
disappear as if drunk by a ghost
— or did he? or was he — ever
in love with her —
his intolerable dear friends
their intolerable dear conversation
among the thunder
& from some puzzling distance —
the pimp eyeing him in the toilet stall .
chewing a marzipan coffin offers him
a stone — here,
clean yourself with this —
talk of love, talk of war
& a dark symbolic horse rears up
against the storm
eyeballs blazing.

The Farolito is deserted
except for a one-legged rooster
& a sleeping dog. The street
empties like a drain
into the *barranco*
where they threw the Consul's body.
Where they also throw
dead dogs & those they do not name
*compañero*, but rather,
*pelado*. Thief.

Bix Beiderbecke at noon.
Alternating sonoryl and straight gin,
five, ten, twenty
versions of a sentence
annealed to one broken one.
Could be anywhere — the same sea
surrounds. Triumphant lucidity
of mind, the hand steady.
Everything behind him now.
*The Voyage That Never Ends*
swells by a page or two,
drifts north-northwest.

Restless. Sonoryl.
Vitamin B. The heebie-jeebies.
Sleep for 3 hours dreaming
animals. *Dear Albert,*
*there's at least 2000 pages more*
*of stuff.* Forgive me.
I am murdered by the pistils
of mauve orchids in a white vase
while bolshevik choirs sing
religious. Strychnine. Allonal.
A cumulo-nimbus cloud of
empty bottles builds in the sky,
the bruises French wine
the shiny spots mescal.
A woman eats a whole man
a man whole in the lurid light.
*Forgive the tone of injured innocence,*
*but.* Chloral. Straight rum.
Nosebleed like an opened tap
pouring into my hands, tossed
like roses at the cheering crowd.
Sodium pentathol — I wake up
weeping the whole grief of the world
strangling my vocabulary.

Loathing Margerie
I would be dead
without her. I guess
I'd better let them
put me in the hospital
for a rest. Every day
she comes to see me
wearing high heels &
reading me censored letters.
Stayed put till I couldn't
stand it, went out one night,
a few days later
I'm in a white bed
dictating memories
to the doctor. Some of them
are pretty good
even if untrue.
I need to be told
there's a reason for this
some word that will describe me
& set me free.

For a few days
I considered having the lobotomy
but Margerie & I
figured it was a bit extreme
& I'd never write again,
no never again.
I'd be in the past tense.

To be rescued from hell
you have to be in hell
so they put me
in some laboratory of it
& sit outside taking notes
every time I scream
nightmare & vomit.
Unlimited supply of gin
interrupted by injections
of apomorphine, a red lightbulb
burning constantly *to increase
the horror effect*, he tells us
over his clipboard.
I was locked in.
Got so damn thirsty
I drank my own piss,
went so crazy there's no words
for it except I saw angels
on fire & so vile
they were laughing at me.
It wasn't so bad.
Outlasted the guy before me
by five days the first time,
sixteen the next. Told them —
the stupid bastards —
I'd had the best time of my life.

The poets' lake country
the final cure,
sheep in pastures grazing
& Wordsworth's daffodils
exactly the host
he said they were — oh bleak
bleak days of separation
from self & catastrophic
states of mind.
He writes with a brave face
to the old fisherman in Dollarton
birthday wishes & fondest love.
They have found a lovely cottage
in the quiet village of Ripe
& listen to music on the radio
& walk and talk with the neighbours
sometimes,
go to The Lamb for a pint
or two or twenty —
it makes no difference.
Alone in the garden
after a violent night
he kisses the bright pink faces
of peonies along the fence
tasting bees & the hereafter.

you say you a wrider
but we read all your wridings
dey dont make sense
you no wrider
you an espider

*where I am it is dark*

A lot of rain falling
& wasted days
but a few gins
& I can still get off
a decent letter.
My personality comes & goes
like the mailman, however
& I can honestly admit
(at my age, how embarrassing)
that I have no idea
who I am. Was always
good at sea, though.
Without a storm
I'm useless.
Other than those
literary parties in New York
where they loved me,
they loved me not
there's one thing
keeps coming back:
we're on our way
to the ferry terminal,
black hangover & arguing
inlet to the left beating off
the morning stars & Margerie
suddenly quiet
puts her hands over her face
& starts to laugh. And somehow
it all seems so comical.

sideways conspiracy
detonates
all things for the mouth
shattered
sucking mother night
claimed
earth & stars, sea & fire
still
a mockingbird pipes
the morning in